FAITH PLC
professed lived celebrated

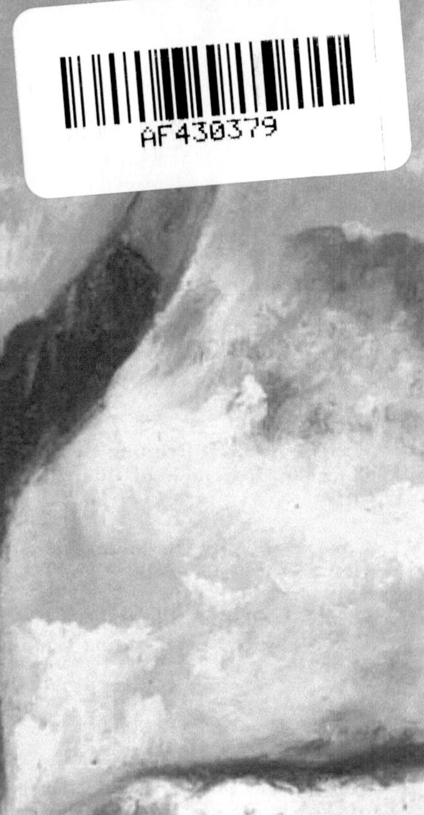

PeterPaul Akinsola Akinola

Nihil Obstat:
Rev. Fr. Paul Olawoore
Catholic Diocese of Oyo, Nigeria
Censor Deputatus

Imprimatur:
Most Rev. Gabriel 'Leke Abegunrin
Archbishop of Ibadan, Nigeria

©2014 by FCM Printing Company
Marcallo, Provincia di Milano
Italy

Cover design by Oladokun Michael Abiodun
OlandoAbbey Concept

Printed and bound in Italy
Published by FCM Printing Company
Marcallo. Italy.

ISBN 974-243-508-4

DEDICATION

This book is lovingly dedicated to all my teachers, mentors and friends in the faith...

To my parents Michael and Mercy Akinola who by words of mouth and example of lives taught me what it means to be a Christian. Also to Emeritus Bishop Julius Babatunde Adelakun, Archbishop Gabriel Leke Abegunrin and Bishop Emmanuel Ade' Badejo my spiritual fathers.

To Patrick, Francis, Helen, James, Mary, Felicia and Cecilia my siblings who by thier accompaniment through thick and thin spur me on in the path of faith.

To all my Parish Priests whose preachings and witness of life stand as nourishment to my faith life. To my catechists both living and dead, Mr. Akinjogunla Sam (RIP), Mr. Nwogu (RIP) and Mr. Alake who impacted in me the basics of faith life.

To my brothers and friends, Kenneth, Anthony, Charles, Victor, Cyril, Martin, Emmanuel, Anthony Muyiwa, Francis, Felix, Francis, David and Thomas in whose company I constantly deepen my faith.

To members of the SSYM who constantly challenge me to practical Christianity. You are all very special to me.

ACKNOWLEDGMENTS

In everyone's life, at some time, our inner fire goes out. It is then burst into flame by an encounter with another human being. We should all be thankful for those people who rekindle the inner spirit. (Albert Schweitzer)

I would like to recognize the contributions of all those without whose assistance this work might not have seen the light of the day. Above all, I am grateful to God Almighty who in His infinite mercy reveals Himself to me, as unworthy as I am. May He be forever praised.

In a special way, I appreciate my big brothers and sister Frs. Peter Adeyemi, Boniface Wuraola and Sr. Regina Oke who took the pain to read through the manuscript, making necessary corrections where needed. To Frs. Kenneth Adesina and Martin Badejo, who are never tired of my continuos disturbance and in whose presence issues regarding the faith and catechesis are discussed, I say a big THANK YOU!

To the families of Akinola 1 & 2 and the Adejuwons for their fraternal support, I am grateful. Special appreciation also goes to Renato, Santina and Dario, Roberto and Sonia and my friends Alesandro and his wife Giulia.

For their financial and moral contributions towards the publishing of this work, I am indebted to all those who have rendered their assistance. In conclusion, I greatly appreciate the support of Frs. Riccardo Brena and Riccardo Dell'Aqua for their fraternal presence and the entire people of Marcallo con Casone for providing the enabling enviroment that helped in the realization of this work.

FOREWORD

In Christian Religious Education, sharing of experience happens to be one of the quite convincing ways of passing across the themes of faith. Due to the fact that faith is a response to the Word of God, it has both ecclesial and personal dimensions. Indeed faith education does not involve just the action of conveying religious information, but the proclamation of the word of God. True. The substantial content of religious education revolves around the Kingdom of God. Yet the subject of that substantial content remains Jesus himself. And following his approach of explaining this substantial content, we find concrete instances of the personal dimension pouring out into and strengthening the ecclesial body. In simpler terms, let us put it that the capacity to know and witness to the truth, has been a very wonderful part of and still renders a great deal in religious education.

The Creed of the Christian Church defined as early as the fourth century at the Council of Nicea and further elaborated at the Council of Constatinople, comes explained in this practical work. Fr. Peter Akinola employs the tool of the personal dimension of the faith to contribute to the understanding of the profession of faith, from where he moves to the aspect of the practical elements which enable the profession of the faith; the sacraments. The third level of discussion takes him to render suggestions on practical actions, so that what is professed, and enabled will become realised. This easy-to-use piece bears a lot on the scriptures, much so that one is tempted to align it with the affirmation of Joseph Ratzinger (later Pope Benedict XVI), when he said that, 'properly speaking, God himself must be the subject of theology.' He further says, 'therefore scripture alone is theology in the fullest sense of the word because it has God as its subject; it does not just speak of him. It is his own speech.'

Frankly speaking, the simplicity of this work makes it accessible to provide a possible approach to faith sharing. An aspect of this is how the writer picks each theme from the background of his own experience yet is able to invite the reader into a silent dialogue which communicates profoundly. That indeed is what faith sharing is much more about. So the apostles commented when Jesus had disappeared from their sight after he broke the bread, "were not our

hearts burning within us while He was speaking to us on the road, while He was explaining the Scriptures to us?" (Luke 24:32).
I conclude with the words of Mary Oliver in one her poetry collections titled Red Bird. She says it is important to, pay attention, be astonished, tell about it. These steps are not just simple instructions to live a life, but in this work, I find a good articulation of attention, astonishment and telling about the Christian faith experience in the mode of its affirmations, its constructive elements and its utilisation.

Sr. Regina Oke (SSMA)

"Il concilio di Trento", Pasquale Cati (1588)

PART I
FAITH PROFESSED

CHAPTER 1

FAITH PROFESSED

Goals are meant to be set in every aspect of human life, so as not to be stagnant. It is the conviction in this sentence that served as the driving force for me, when at the very beginning of the Year of Faith, declared by Pope Benedict XVI (Oct. 11, 2012 – Nov. 14, 2013), I decided to re-explore what exactly is it that I believe and what are my grounds for believing in it.

Even though faith is a free gift of God, it requires the duty of a response. Such a response to faith is not a one-time action, but an all-time thing, which calls for a continuous action of examination and re-examination. The reason is not far-fetched. It is simply because a faith that is not explored and re-explored stands the risk of becoming fanatical on one side or lapsed on the other side. Consequently, having received the gift of faith, primarily from God and through the channel of the community of God's people, there is the need, especially on a personal level, to consistently examine the object of faith in relation to the response which is given to the demands of faith. Like many other realities of man's life, many try to avoid the challenge of making a profound search into the significance of their faith, probably for the fear of not being thrown off balance in matters of the faith practice. Hence they remain on the same level for a time. But because the choice of being static always carries mediocrity with itself, the unexamined faith stands the risk of getting off-track gradually.

The questions of Jesus to His disciples "who do people say I am?", and "... you, who do you say I am?" (cf. Matt 16:13,15) are ready pointers to the fact that faith has to be examined in view of coming to its better appreciation. The Year of Faith afforded me the opportunity to once again re-examine my faith. Hence this I have tried to put down in clear, ordinary language. The aim is for it to serve as both a challenge for others to also share their faith, and an insight to those searching for the reasons for the hope they have in them. At the end of it all, I have a deep feeling within me of sharing the fruit of my reflection with all those who may need such since without being testified to, faith remains not useful.

Will this little work say anything new? I doubt it. However, I am sure it will get someone to think further, it will prompt in someone the need to consider more profoundly the little details of faith which ordinarily we profess, celebrate and live, sometimes without deep considerations for our convictions.

CHAPTER 2

I BELIEVE IN GOD

Professing our faith is not something new to many of us, if only for the fact that at every Sunday Eucharistic celebration, as a community of God's people, we make and concentrate on the liturgical action of professing the same faith in and through which we were baptized and become sons and daughters of God.

Faith! What is faith? I have decided not to consult any dictionary but to sincerely give my personal understanding of the word; Faith to me is a conviction that is personal but at the same time has its basis in the community. It is a deep trust that keeps the world moving and without it, no one, I repeat no one, can live a minute longer! But, wait a minute; am I making any sense even to myself? What of the numerous world acclaimed atheists? Hmmm, there stands the confusion - no 'atheist' to my knowledge has ever claimed not to have faith, they only doubt the reality of a particular mode of existence of an object of faith. Every man is born a believer, we only grow up learning to disbelieve!

Here comes another dimension to the question of faith. If I say I believe or that I am convinced or that I have deep trust, I must go ahead to ask myself; 'In who/what rests my belief? If I am the subject that believes, then there must necessarily be an object of belief. As a Christian, my immediate answer is God! That is why I profess always the creed of the community of God's people, that is, the Church, which begins with the affirmation that 'I believe in God the Almighty Father'.

Attention! Who is God? The answer rests in the second part of my professed faith. He is the Almighty Father! Thus, God = The Almighty Father = Is the One in whom I believe. My use of the word Father is not limited to a gender, rather it is a conceptual usage. While I probably have an earthly father who makes this description unquestionably suitable, I also know that there are many whose experiences of earthly fathers do not allow a faith in the father figure God. The Father Almighty for me is a perfection of the father figure that we all have. When one says 'my father is not responsible', it is exactly because such has a conception of who a father ought to be and it is a defection of this that leads to the idea of 'Irresponsible fatherhood'.

A father is expected to be a guide, a protector, a teacher, a motivator, a refuge, a provider, a source of hope, a model etc. The perfection of all these is who my God, the object of my faith is! That is why He is ALMIGHTY. If He is ALMIGHTY, then He must be beyond and ahead of every other, in such a way that all look up to Him and submit under His authority and so I say; I believe in ONE GOD, THE FATHER ALMIGHTY!

LET US PRAY

Father Almighty, the One and Only God
I thank You for the gift of Your self-revelation
give me the grace, to come to a deeper understanding
of You and to be an instrument of making you known
to all and sundry in my words and my deeds.
May those who trust in You not be put to shame through me O Lord.
This we ask through Christ our Lord. Amen

CHAPTER 3

I BELIEVE IN JESUS CHRIST

In the last chapter, I started this series of self-examination of what I believe. However, the Father whom I believe in, I have never seen! This makes relevant the wordings of that soul lifting Yoruba adoration song:

Mi o ri E ri o, (I have never seen You)

Olorun mi (My God)

Sugbon mo "feel" Re (But I feel You) 2x

"I have a feeling" Olorun mi (I have a feeling my God)

Wipe O waaa! (That You exist!) 2x

How ambiguous then it will be to talk of Him? No wonder many are lost in ascribing His essence to many other beings. But one thing is clear; He is LOVE par excellence and thus it is not surprising to me that all through history, He has revealed Himself to humankind, through one way or the other, though we usually miss the point. Then, at the fullness of time, to remove all excuse of error, He made a self-manifestation in His only begotten Son, and thus, the once Unseen God becomes visible; He eats, drinks, talks, plays and does everything we do (except sin) within history. And so, the Creator of time came to live within time; He who made man, was born of man! In Jesus Christ, the afore-written song becomes debatable because we can now not only feel, but see God!

Yes! I believe in the Son of God who took flesh in the womb of the Virgin Mary. I believe that He is one with the Father and since He is the Word of the Father, it is through Him that everything was made. I believe that in Jesus, God walked and still walks the surface of the earth, that in Him is the Yes and Amen to all our prayers and petitions. I believe that in His name, every knee shall bend and every tongue shall confess. I believe that by His death on the cross, He has paid my ransom and so I am free! Alleluia!!

Attention! Did I just say that God died? Yes! My Lord and God died, He was condemned by mere mortals, He took my curse on Himself. He died not because death has power over Him, but much more because He has to show His superiority over death - and so, He went to death's abode to defeat death! What greater victory can there be? Death was defeated in its very background and now, I can trustfully sing: 'I fear no longer death, my Lord Jesus Christ has driven death out... (Emi ko beru iku, Oluwa Jesu mi, O ti le e jade lo...).

So, death was defeated and on the third day, 'The Author of Life' arose! If He had not risen from the dead, what confidence would we have of our own resurrection too? He lives now, never to die again. To show us that, He will forever live, just before His death, He gave Himself for all those who believe in Him as the Food of Life: 'This is My Body... This is My Blood'. So, He lives continually with us in the Eucharist. Yes I believe! The Word became flesh and He dwelt among us, the same Flesh became Food for our soul by the power of the Word, so that in those who eat of this Food worthily, the Word may once again take Flesh!

Yes and certainly, I believe and I am convinced of my faith, what about you?

LET US PRAY

Almighty Father, you so much love the world
that You sent Your only begotten Son to dwell in our midst
such that all who believe in Him may have everlasting life.
Make me know You and Your Son whom You sent
Give me the grace to enter into a deeper relationship with Jesus,
The Word who became flesh, that through Him, I may
proclaim Your love to the world and dwell forever in
Your presence! I believe Lord, help my unbelief!!!

CHAPTER 4

I BELIEVE IN THE HOLY SPIRIT

What exactly am I saying? My faith is in a God who is Father Almighty, invisible yet ever present, who made Himself known (within history) in His Son, the visible self-manifestation of God. But then, that is not all! I also believe in the Holy Spirit - The Communicating Presence of God. He it is who makes known to as many as are open to Him, the reality of the Father and the Son. He is the Spirit of Truth and in Him there is no danger of falsehood, thus it is, that whenever and wherever He is welcomed, there is LIBERTY. The Holy Spirit is the power of God! It is for this reason that He is able to empower, to set free, to heal and even to raise us from the dead. Alleluia!

Do I then believe in three gods? Capital NO! From the outset, I have made it clear, that my faith is in One God. In actual fact, the idea of three gods is self-defeating for if there are three gods, then they are not gods for none will be supreme. The one I believe in is One God (Godhead) who is three Persons - These three persons are distinct, indivisible persons of the same Godhead. Here comes the 'stupidity' of faith, for how can I be talking of three and yet One? If they are distinct persons, how come they cannot be separated?

Let me start by saying that this is a mystery and it is for that reason that faith is required. Nevertheless, while my faith is beyond mere human reasoning, it is not opposed to reason and thus I will try to illustrate, even when I know that my God is greater than human language and experience. I humbly own up to the inadequacy of my reasoning yet, I will for the sake of those who ask for the reason of the hope I have, give a response, difficult as it is going to be.

Since God (in whom I believe) created everything that exists, in all of creature, I believe, the humble souls can experience and encounter the greatness of God. This I say in the same manner that we experience the 'greatness' of an artist in his art works or the ingenuity of a scientist in what he invents, so also and much more, we experience God in the works of His hand.

We take for example two elements created by God: the first being fire! I am doubly sure that all of us, young and old, male and female have seen fire in whatever form. What I am not sure of is whether we have been attentive enough to notice that in every fire, when observed keenly, there are different 'colours' - blue, yellow, red... (If you have not noticed this before, try and observe it today). Now, whatever colour it is we see, distinct as they are, they make up the same fire! Not only that, but also there is the fact that the distinct colours can never be separated one from the other for it is the same reality.

On the other hand is the illustration said to have been made by an illiterate farmer in the eastern part of Africa. Year in year out, this farmer plants grains, harvests his crops and dries them in a barn for conservation and storage. In this daily activity, he got a 'tick'! The sun it is that dries the grains, but this same sun is up there in the sky (as we say). Its rays it is that fall on us and these rays produce the heat that dries the grain. Hence, this farmer reasons; 'we all know that the ray is distinct from the sun and the heat, so also is the heat from the sun and the ray and the sun from the ray and the heat, but then, can we separate the one from the other? Can we think of one without the others?

As said earlier, no one of us can explain God, but He has revealed Himself to us as a Trinity, distinct yet inseparable and I believe! No wonder God is Love, for how can He be an Indivisible Community if not that He is Love? No wonder the greatest need of man is love for we are created in the image and likeness of Love!

LET US PRAY

O perfect LOVE; Father, Son and Holy Spirit,
I thank You for revealing Yourself to me.
Even though I still see as through a veil,
and my knowledge still imperfect, I believe!
I invite you O Holy Trinity, to reveal Yourself more to me,
and grant me the grace to make You known even to
the ends of the earth.
I believe Lord, help my unbelief! Amen

CHAPTER 5

I BELIEVE IN THE CHURCH

In the past three chapters, I have tried to express my faith in the Triune God, I have employed very clear language (I think) in doing this in order to express how plain my faith is to me; I live it, drink it, eat it and breathe it! I have not pretended that what I say expresses absolutely the subject of my faith, for thence, I wonder why it would be called faith. But, I am so glad and contented that I know Him in Whom I believe.

How did I arrive at all this knowledge? How come I am this convinced of my faith? How did I come to this level of assent? The answer is clear and direct; through The Church. Yes, The Church and not just a church; that assembly of God's people whose 'foundation' the Lord Jesus Christ built on the faith of Peter. The Church that is the Body of Christ! And again, I dare to say; I believe in the Church.

I have heard a lot of people tell me that they believe in God but not in The Church. This sounds somewhat nonsensical to me, for how do you believe a message but not the messenger? The authenticity of any message rests a lot on our perception of the messenger. Anyway, I am not here to discuss the faith of others, but my own faith and the reason for it, I believe in The Church that is One, Holy, Catholic and Apostolic.

When I say One, I mean that Church, which is visibly under one physical head, that is, the Vicar of Christ on earth. I hold to the teachings of the Church as expressed in Her magisterium because the Lord Jesus Christ has promised to be with the Church until the end of time and I believe! This same Church is locally represented in every diocese by the bishop, who is in communion with the Vicar of Christ and in every parish by the Parish Priest who also maintains that union with the Pope, through his Bishop.

That I say the Church is Holy is not because her members, are not weak and sinful people, but because the teachings of the Church is holy. Much more, because Her Head, the Lord Jesus Christ is Holy and from Him and by the power of the Holy Spirit flows holiness down through the Church. Even though the physical Church, the Church Militant is filled with weak humans, sinners, but they are sinners with a difference, they are sinners seeking to become saints and join the Church Triumphant!

That the Church is Catholic is proper in the sense of the word - Universal. In obedience to the promptings of Her Master, the Church goes even to the ends of the world, proclaiming the gospel of salvation. It is not just at a corner of a village claiming to be worldwide! Its membership is not restricted to race or colour, but to all who accept the teachings of the gospel and dispose themselves to be baptized, they become sons and daughters of the Church of Christ, members of His Body.

Lastly, I say the Church is Apostolic, for it is built on the foundation of the Apostles! It has a direct succession from Jesus, to St. Peter and down to the present Pope! It is not a Church that came into existence by mere dreams or personal vision. It was intended by Christ, when He called His apostles and named Simon as Peter, the Rock on which the Church would be built. As Eve was formed from the side of Adam, so also this Church was formed on the Cross of Calvary through the instrumentality of the Blood and Water that flowed from the side of Christ! On the day of Pentecost, the Church was publicly made known by the Apostles after they had received the gift of the Holy Spirit, the Spirit of Truth. In this Church, I believe, I do not know about you.

LET US PRAY

Father in heaven, Your only Begotten Son,
Our Lord Jesus Christ, within His mission in
the world formed the Church to be a Sacrament
of His continuous presence in the world.
Grant the I may believe more in Your Church,
That I may be able to make use of the graces
You daily bequeath to me through the Church
And through these graces, may I be drawn more
and more to Your mercy and presence.
Through Christ, our Lord. Amen

CHAPTER 6

I BELIEVE IN THE COMMUNION OF SAINTS...

The age long thirst of man is to live forever; not to go into extinction. Why would he not thirst for this, since he is created in the image and likeness of the Immortal God? My faith tells me that in Christ Jesus, I will live forever because He (Jesus Christ), to whom I have been united by virtue of my faith and His grace, lives forever! Thus, I believe in the Communion of saints, the forgiveness of sin, the resurrection of the dead and life everlasting. Alleluia! Praise the Lord!!

By the communion of the saints, I believe that together with all those who have gone before me marked with the sign of faith, we form the same Church; the same body of Christ! Thus, I am never alone and never act alone, the entire Church of Christ is always with me. The three realities of the Church always accompany me, namely, the Church Triumphant (Those who behold the fullness of beatific vision, comprising of the Saints, Martyrs and Angels), The Suffering Church (The Holy Souls in Purgatory) and the Church Militant (Those of us who are on pilgrimage towards our eternal home with Christ Jesus, the Head of the Church). Thus even if physically I mourn the death of a beloved in Christ, my faith tells me it is not a loss but gain, for we are ever united, never to part again.

But how do we participate in the full life of He who is without sin? We are humans; weak and fragile, every now and then, we do not measure up to expectation. I believe that the mercy of God is greater than my sins. That every time I return to Him with a penitent heart and a firm resolve to avoid sin, He is ever ready to forgive me; and why not, since He is LOVE, who does not rejoice in evil but pardons all faults. Hence, I believe in the forgiveness of sins.

Christ Jesus rose from the dead, never to die again! For this reason, I believe that death is not the end of the journey, rather a passage to a more glorious life. If Christ had not died and risen, I would be the greatest fool to believe this; no wonder the devil tempted Him again on the Cross of Calvary to come down from the Cross if He is the Christ; a repetition of the temptation to jump down from the heights at the beginning of His public ministry. Alas! Once again the devil was defeated and Jesus won the battle, for He remained on the Cross till death and He rose again, for no one can destroy the Temple of Christ, which is His body. I believe in the resurrection of the dead! Indeed because Jesus rose, we; believers in Him, members of His body will also resurrect!

Having resurrected, we shall live forever because death has been rendered powerless. Thus, again, I profess that I believe in Life Everlasting, a life that is lived in Jesus Christ, who Himself is Life. It is the same Jesus Christ who has made known this truth of faith because He Himself is The Truth and in Him, only in Him, all these are possible because He is The Way.

I believe, Lord help my unbelief!

LET US PRAY

Eternal Rock of Ages, The Way, The Truth and The Life
grant to me today, the grace to walk in You and to know You,
that in You, I may have life;
For You have said that You came to give us life, life in abundance.
Make me a partaker of the life, O Lord,
and grant me the grace to always stand on the part of life
against the culture of death.
Do not allow the concerns of this material world
to draw me away from Your presence.
Jesus, Son of the Living God, I trust in You.
Amen.

CHAPTER 7

CLOSING REMARKS

You might have faithfully followed the trend of my assent to faith in the last five chapters and for that, I say a very big thank you for the effort.

I have chosen to start from this perspective because I know that nobody can live or give what he does not have in the first instance. You might have heard a lot of people saying 'I believe just in Jesus Christ and I do not bother myself with all these doctrines' or 'what matters is faith in Jesus and not doctrine'. Let it be known that all those who say such are actually suffering from some sort of spiritual astigmatism, for even the statement itself 'I believe in Jesus', immediately prompts us to further question; 'Who is Jesus?'. Thus it was, that even Jesus during His historico-physical earthly sojourn asked of His disciples a two-in-one question; who do people/you say I Am? (Matt 16:13ff). In this question is contained a request for comprehension of who God is (I Am), who Jesus is. Little wonder that it is on the correct apprehension of who Jesus is, that He built His Church - the faith of the apostles as professed by St. Peter!

The focal point of the creed is Jesus Christ, for the reason that it is in Him that we see the God whom no eye can see (Ex 33:20) face to face as God took the flesh of man and dwelt among us!(Heb 1:1, Jn 1:14). In Him, the Son, we come to know God as Father (cf Jn 10:30-33), and in Him, we are introduced to the Holy Spirit (Jn 14:16,26). In fact, Jesus made us see the Oneness of the Three Person (cf Matt 28:19-20)! Furthermore, it is in Jesus that we come to know His Body the Church, the sacraments and the reality of resurrection. As usual, if you want to know more about your faith, come to Jesus and see (Jn 1:46)!

You will notice that before now, I have intentionally not made explicit biblical references, the reason is clear; if you do not believe in the Church as revealed to us by Jesus Christ, you cannot claim to believe in the Bible, for it is a 'compilation' of the faith of the Church.

Another fact worthy of mention is that we have basically two versions of the same creed, that is, the Apostles' Creed and the Nicene Creed, which we pray during our liturgical gatherings and in some other individual prayers. In the Apostles' Creed, the opening sentence is 'I believe...', while in the Nicene's, it is 'We believe...'. These in no way tamper with the substance of the creed which is one and the same in both. In fact, to me it is a way of saying 'I believe in what the Church believes'. The creed is in no way a source of controversy, but on the other hand, it is a compilation of the answers of faith given at the moments of controversies (1 Pet 3:15). Hence it affords us the opportunity to know the One, in whom we believe.

Are you still having doubts about your faith? I will recommend that you prayerfully say the Creed again, asking the Holy Spirit, the Spirit of Truth to open your heart, mind and intellect that you may come to a fuller understanding of the gift of faith which the Lord has given you and within the community of God's children, to be able to celebrate it.

LET US PRAY

We believe in one God,
the Father, the Almighty,
Maker of all that is, seen and unseen.
We believe in one Lord, Jesus Christ,
the only Son of God,
eternally begotten of the Father,
God from God, Light from Light,
true God from true God,
begotten, not made,
of one Being with the Father.
Through him all things were made.
For us and for our salvation
he came down from heaven:
by the power of the Holy Spirit
he became incarnate from the Virgin Mary,
and was made man.
For our sake he was crucified under Pontius Pilate;
he suffered death and was buried.
On the third day he rose again
in accordance with the Scriptures;
he ascended into heaven
and is seated at the right hand of the Father.
He will come again in glory to judge the living and the dead,
and his kingdom will have no end.
We believe in the Holy Spirit, the Lord, the giver of life,

who proceeds from the Father and the Son.
With the Father and the Son he is worshipped and glorified.
He has spoken through the Prophets.
We believe in one holy catholic and apostolic Church.
We acknowledge one baptism for the forgiveness of sins.
We look for the resurrection of the dead,
and the life of the world to come. Amen.

"Seven Sacraments", altarpiece,
Rogier van der Weyden (1445-1450)

24

PART II
FAITH CELEBRATED

CHAPTER 8

THE CELEBRATIONS

It is with great pleasure that I welcome you to the second part of our Faith journey series. In this section, we shall be taking an journey into the theme "Celebrated Faith" after our little excursion into 'Faith Professed'. Having established what the main content of the faith is, we shall be looking into how the faith is to be celebrated, but firstly we need to ask; what is celebration? The word celebration which is a noun, is from the verb 'to celebrate'. It has its root in the Latin word celebrare, meaning 'to attend', 'to frequent'. Within this sense, to celebrate our faith will amount to attending/frequenting the different media of professing the faith.

It is thus practically impossible to celebrate the faith in the absence of the Church, which serves the mediatory role of making known the reality of the Holy Trinity! In fact as already pointed out in the first part, faith in the Church is the fourth article of faith out of the seven in the Nicene creed. Hence it is through the Church that we come to a better knowledge of the Trinity, which we find in the first three articles and of which we are guided and taught in the last three articles!

Before Jesus' ascension as recorded in the gospel according to St. Matthew, He promised to be with the disciples until the end of time (Matt 28:20). But many may ask; how did this come to fulfillment since Jesus physically ascended into heaven? The reality is that before His departure, the Lord Jesus Christ had given efficacious signs of His continuous presence, to His disciples, who are the foundation stones of His Body, The Church. These efficacious signs are referred to as Sacraments. It is in the frequenting of these sacraments that we celebrate our faith.

The admonition of the scriptures, not to forsake the assembly of the brethren is actually a call to this (cf. Heb. 10:25). It is a call to follow the example of the apostles in gathering to celebrate the Word and the sacraments; realities that give evidence to the real presence of Jesus with His people (cf Act 2:42). It is worthy to note here, that the word, important as it is, leads more to the burning of hearts than recognizing the resurrected Lord (cf Lk 24: 29-32)! You might also have heard of many who say; the Church will not save you. To this, I beg to disagree, because statements like this come as a result of beclouded knowledge of what the Church is. Since salvation comes through and only through Christ, it will be paradoxical for anyone to say the Church cannot save, for the Church is the Body of Christ (cf Eph 5:23)!

It is actually more of a truth that the Church is not a guarantee of salvation, just as it is well known that even with the gift of salvation that Jesus brought for us, many will still opt out themselves, not to make heaven. It is this that gives credence to the words of St. Augustine of Hippo that 'God who created us without us, cannot save us without us'. Like the Ark of Noah, the Church is the Ark of salvation, but it is so, only for those who will be ready to follow her precepts and enter before the deluge of destruction. It is for this reason that she (The Church) is called Mater et Magister (Mother and Teacher).

In the following pages, we shall be looking into how to celebrate our faith which implies more or less to how we shall attend/frequent the Church and thus come into a deeper relationship with the Lord Jesus Christ, the Author and Finisher of our faith.

LET US PRAY

Lord Jesus Christ,
Before Your ascension from the earth, You gave us a gift of Your Church,
built on the faith of the apostles.
In the following chapters, we shall be exploring the reality of your Church,
Send unto us Your Holy Spirit, the Spirit of Truth
To lead us to Your fuller Truth
That knowing the Truth, we may be set free.
We ask this through Christ our Lord. Amen.

CHAPTER 9

BAPTISM

In the introduction to this section, our point of conclusion was in asserting that through the Church, Christ saves! This He does through various means but above all through the sacraments by which He continually makes known His ever present reality with His body, the Church. Here we come once again with 'terminologies' (extra biblical as they use to say), but what do we mean to say by 'sacrament'? The word sacrament is from the Latin word sacramentum which is from the verb sacrare meaning 'to consecrate'. Further, this word, consecrate means in English language, to set apart/dedicate/make sacred. Flowing from this, it would be real ignorance for anyone to still maintain that the word sacrament is an extra Biblical invention of the Church. Instead, we should realize that the sacraments are the visible signs, instituted by Jesus Christ by which we are consecrated more unto him. The age long beautiful catechism refers to a sacrament as "the outward sign of inward grace ordained by Jesus Christ, by which grace is given to our souls."

In the following lines, we shall look into how we frequent Christ's presence (celebrate cf. last chapter) through the sacrament of Baptism.

Has it ever occurred to you that to be a partaker of the eternal life offered by Jesus, He explicitly recommended two actions? The first is what we are looking into now, for Jesus, in His nocturnal conversation with Nicodemus said ' unless one is born of water and spirit, he cannot enter the kingdom of God' (Cf Jn 3:1-6). This kingdom initiates from here on earth in the reality of the Church. When we celebrate the solemnity of Christ the King annually, we affirm that He has a kingdom and that we are citizens of that kingdom! However, we must always remember this saying of Jesus that it is the re-birth which comes from the water and the spirit that serves as our 'visa' to entering this kingdom.

Just before ascending to heaven, the Lord Jesus Christ further commanded His disciples (physical representatives of the Church for all ages) to make disciples of all nation, teach and baptize them into the Trinity! (cf Matt 28:18-19). It is for this reason that I consider baptism as the most important of all sacraments because it is the 'Gateway Sacrament' without which nobody has a right of passage to any other sacrament.

In the Church, baptism is defined as that sacrament which cleanses us from original sin, makes us Christians, children of God and members of the Church! What a great gift this sacrament is then! It cleanses us from every attachment to the kingdom of darkness (cf. Col 1:13-14), that is why in baptism we publicly reject Satan and all his works and empty promises and make a public declaration for and to the Holy Trinity.

This re-birth (being born again) is a once and for all decision but needs to be daily renewed and examined. If I have opted for the life of grace, then it becomes expedient for me to daily re-dedicate myself to this reality and not allow the distractions of this world to snatch me away from my goal. Once we have been baptized, and thus become sons and daughters of God, then like children we have the responsibility to project the image of the family, and baptism reminds us also of this when with the oil of Chrism, we are anointed to participate in the three offices of Christ our Saviour, that is, the Priestly, Kingly and Prophetic offices of Jesus.

As priests (common priesthood of believers), we are called to offer ourselves daily as a living sacrifice, holy and acceptable to the Lord (cf. Rm 12:1ff). As kings, we are called upon to live our lives with dignity as it befits the children of God (1 Pet 2:9,10) and as prophets, called to announce the good news of the kingdom (cf Jer 1:5, Lk 4:18, 1 Cor 9:16).

The baptismal challenge is for us to daily examine how faithful we keep to these callings which are the gifts we received when we were baptized and the responsibilities they bestow on us.

LET US PRAY

Father in heaven,
You loved me so much that in Jesus Christ,
Your only begotten Son, and by the grace of
baptism, You have made me Your adopted son/daughter,
and a citizen of Your kingdom.
Open my eyes of faith o Lord,
That I may come to a deeper understanding
of the graces of baptism.
Grant that I may receive the grace of faithfulness
to my baptismal promises and a daily renewal of
the same in my life.
This I ask, through Jesus Christ our Lord.
Amen.

CHAPTER 10

THE EUCHARIST

Brethren in Christ, we established earlier that to be a partaker in the eternal life for which the Son of God became man (Jn 1:14, 10:10b), Jesus explicitly recommended two actions. The first of which is Baptism which we have treated. Now, our focus shifts to the second action, which is the Holy Eucharist. Hear what Jesus had to say:

...truly, truly I say to you, unless you eat the flesh of the Son of man and drink His blood, you have no life in you; he who eats my flesh and drinks my blood has eternal life and I will raise him up on the last day. For my flesh is food indeed, and my blood is drink indeed (Jn. 6:53-55).

It is a generally held fact that we become what we eat, this explains why nutritionists recommend always, a balanced diet for physical wellbeing. On the other hand, Jesus' saving work is above all oriented towards our spiritual wellbeing and thus He sets forth to feed our souls with the spiritual balanced diet of His body and blood in the Eucharist. Even while He continues to cater for physical needs, it is oriented towards giving a right perspective to the spiritual reality!

In my reflections on the Eucharist, I am always drawn to how Jesus began His teachings from physical food and drink (what I call the 'meal/table ministry' of Jesus)! In actual fact, it was during an encounter with a 'kegite'* group that the inspiration of this first came to me; during this encounter in which I was admonishing my friends who were members to be cautious, they replied me by singing a song that I still remember vividly. It goes thus;

Ni Galili, fellow Jesus s'omi d'oti (3x)

(At Galilea, comrades, Jesus turned water into wine)

O ni k'a maa mu lo k'a si ma yo

(He said we should continue to drink it and be happy)

Ma ya, ma ya e, ma ya, ma ya, ma ya, ma ya (3x)

O ni k'a maa mu lo k'a si ma yo!

This song which is a reference to the second chapter of the gospel according to St. John (2:1-9), puts the reason for continuous drinking of wine (sometimes excessive which the Church does not support) to the fact that Jesus performed a miracle of changing water to wine! The point that my friends fail to realize is the fact that wine was not the end product of the sign performed by Jesus, but that He later did turn the wine into His blood and only at this point did He command us to do it in memory of Him! (cf 1Cor 11:25)

In the same vein, the miracle of the multiplication of bread drew many to Christ. In actual fact, they were searching for Him to make Him king for this purpose (cf. Jn 6:1-15). Instead, the physical bread was a pointer to a greater reality for the end product is that it be turned to His body (cf Matt 26:26ff, Mk 14:22-25, Lk 22:19-20). Thus, Christ gave us the sacrament of His body and blood, which from the earliest beginnings of His Church has been the raison d'etre of their gathering (cf Acts 2:42).

The Holy Eucharist is the true body and blood of our Lord Jesus Christ, together with His soul and divinity, under the appearance of bread and wine. It is the sacrament of our becoming one with Christ (as earlier said, we become what we eat) and since baptism sets our feet on the pilgrimage of faith, the Eucharist is the food for the pilgrimage (cf 1 King 19:7). If only we will be conscious of He, Who we receive in the Eucharist, how blessed and humbled we shall become (cf. 1 Cor. 11:28-32, 2 Cor. 4:7).

The celebration of the Eucharist (Mass) makes real, over and over, the merit of the sacrifice of Calvary in which Christ Jesus became our Paschal lamb, the same one that John the Baptist pointed to as He, who takes away the sins of the world (cf Jn 1.29). At every Mass, heaven is joined to earth and we have a free passage to be in the presence of God! Dear brothers and sisters, why then on earth should we miss such an opportunity and not come together to celebrate the mystery of our salvation?

LET US PRAY

Eucharistic Lord,
You who have made yourself available to and for us
As Food for the nourishment and deliverance of our souls,
Grant that we may come to a better awareness
Of the love you manifest for us, when you decided
To continually remain with us, Your Church
In the Eucharistic Species.
May our reception of You today and always, bring us to life everlasting
We ask for this and many other graces,
Through Christ our Lord. Amen.

CHAPTER 11

CONFIRMATION

In this chapter, I am actually torn between two mysteries. Ordinarily, after last chapter's discussion on the Eucharist, I am tempted to treat herein, the sacrament of Reconciliation, considering the intrinsic link that exists between the two. On the other hand, it sounds rational to me to just move on and discuss as a whole the sacraments of initiation, in which case the sacrament of Confirmation has to come next. After much thought, I have opted for the sacrament of Confirmation for this chapter.

The Baltimore Catechism defines Confirmation as the sacrament through which the Holy Spirit comes to us in a special way and enables us to profess our faith as strong and perfect Christians and soldiers of Jesus Christ. Its basis is found in the admonition and promise of Jesus Christ to send the Holy Spirit on believers (Cf. Jn. 14:16, 15:26,16:7, Act 1:8). This sacrament is closely linked with the sacrament of Baptism but more directed towards mission!

It is disheartening to see the number of confirmed Catholics today who do not know or are reluctant to carry out the task towards which the Sacrament is intended. What is this task and how are we to adequately prepare ourselves to benefit of it?

The Holy Spirit and Confirmation: In the sacrament of Confirmation, we receive in a special way, the presence and manifestations of the Holy Spirit. The same Spirit through whom we were adopted as sons and daughters in the sacrament of Baptism, empowers us in the sacrament of Confirmation to witness to Christ! At this juncture, it is necessary to say that in the Early Church, the three sacraments of Baptism, Confirmation and Holy Eucharist are administered together. Whereas due to the fact that now, baptism is administered to little children, the Church allows that Confirmation be administered after. In actual fact, the law of the Church states that it should be administered "at about the age of discretion unless the conference of bishops has determined another age" (Can 891).

It is thus not surprising that many Episcopal conferences have chosen a later date considering the fact of mission which the sacrament requests from the recipient. This does not mean that little children cannot be involved in the mission of the Church, but the more 'obvious' missions are reserved, for existential reason to grown-ups.

Since we expect the Holy Spirit in a particularly special manner with the reception of the sacrament of Confirmation, it is expedient that we prepare adequately for this reception by way of instructions and prayers! Even the apostles, together with the Blessed Virgin Mary were in prayers for nine days in preparation for the Holy Spirit. I say this because the 'inadequacy' of our catechesis is visible in the many confirmed Catholics who were actually not prepared adequately, neither by way of prayers nor by instruction! The mission task of Confirmation: ... you will receive power when the Holy Spirit come upon you, and you will be my witness... (Act 1:8). This quotation from the Acts of the Apostles is essential to our understanding of the sacrament of Confirmation; it confers power but for the purpose of witnessing! Thus, if after receiving this sacrament, you find yourself still timid or unable to witness to Christ, there is something fundamentally wrong. You are not yet a matured Christian if you cannot witness I must tell you. That is why the sacrament of Confirmation seals the initiation process as a Christian. I am always convinced of the three levels to being a Christian; one can be among the crowd following Christ, be a disciple or at the peak of followership, be an apostle, that is, one who is sent out as an ambassador of the Master! This is what the sacrament of Confirmation sets to achieve in us Christians. Are you ready for the mission?

LET US PRAY

Send forth Your Spirit, O Lord
And renew the face of the earth.
Make of us a habitation worthy of Your Spirit
And creditable instrument of renewal on the earth.
You have called and chosen us by the power of the
Holy Spirit, and You have mandated us to preach the
Good news, in and out of season;
Grant us the grace to be conscious of the graces
We have received, when the Holy Spirit was given
To us afresh on the day of our confirmation,
That we may live ever with this consciousness
To the greater glory of Your holy name.
We ask this through Christ our Lord. Amen

CHAPTER 12

SACRAMENT OF RECONCILIATION

It is a normal habit for many of us to take stock towards the end of a particular exercise before starting or beginning a new stage. The key word here is taking stock and we shall come back to it in a while. What do we mean to say by the Sacrament of Reconciliation?

Simply put, it is a sacrament in which we receive the grace of forgiveness for the sins we commit after baptism and the grace to live the Christian life in a better manner. This sacrament which can also be called by other names such as Penance and Confession is a sacrament of mercy. It is strictly linked to the sacraments of Baptism and the Holy Eucharist by taking its leave from the former and having its end in the latter. How is this so, you may want to ask. In the sacrament of Baptism, we make a vow, a fundamental decision to reject Satan and all his works and empty promises and to accept Jesus Christ as our personal Lord and Saviour, and as consequence of this acceptance we declare our faith in the Creed (cf. Faith Professed series). What this vow requests of us is, like the Blessed Virgin Mary, to always say;" ...be it done to me according to your word" and to always put on our lips the words of the prayer our Lord taught us; "Your will be done on earth". In doing this, we maintain our relationship with the Lord, He remains our God and we, His people (cf Ex 6:7, Lev 26:12, Jer 30:22).

Instead, many a time, for the reason of our weakness and taking away our gaze from the Saviour, we fall into sin, that is, a disobedience to God's directive and we tend to hide ourselves from His presence (cf. Gen 3:8). In this state, the indelible mark of our Baptism, by and through which we have been made children of God, calls us to awareness that we are not meant to live in the bondage of sin but in freedom of the sons and daughters of God (cf. Lk 15:16-18).

To re-attain this liberation, from the power and clutches of sin, the Lord Jesus Christ has given us the sacrament of Reconciliation, made obvious when after His resurrection, He gave His disciples the power to forgive sins (or retain it) (Cf. Jn 20:19-23). Thus, we see the takeoff point of the sacrament of Reconciliation based on the freedom we have received by virtue of our Baptism.

On the other hand, our goal is to become one with Christ (cf. Gal 4:19) and that is attained in the sacrament of the Holy Eucharist where we receive the Body and Blood, Soul and Divinity of our Lord Jesus Christ under the appearance of bread and wine. However, we cannot participate in this communion unless we clean ourselves of all unrighteousness (cf. Ps 5:5, 1 Cor 11:27-31), which again brings us to the importance of the sacrament of Reconciliation.

Earlier on, I talked about stock taking, yes, that exactly is what the sacrament of Reconciliation needs, that is, that we 'put ourselves on scale' with the commandment of Love and see those areas where we have not measured up to expectation, even with the judgement of our conscience (Examination of Conscience). Then, with a sense of remorse for having transgressed the law of God, who so much loved us and made us His children in Jesus Christ and a firm decision to avoid the repetition of the same actions in future, we proceed to have a sacramental confession of our sins. Mind you dear friend, we are not going before a judge who will punish us for our sins, instead, we approach a loving Father who all the while has been on the lookout for us and is ready to embrace us in His arms and throw a feast for our return from the grip of sin (cf Lk 15:7, 10, 20-24)!

Oh! How wonderful it is to belong to the Church of Christ Himself! Will you deprive yourself of this grace? Will you not approach Him who is ready to save you and give you a brand new beginning? No matter the gravity of your sins, I tell you, the mercy of God is greater (cf. Rm 5:20). What you have to do is to approach the throne of mercy and talk things over with Christ (Cf. Is 1:18). Will you avail yourself of the grace?

LET US PRAY

Merciful God,
You are a Mystery not fully comprehended
For You combine the fullness of Mercy with Justice.
Give us insight into Your mercy, that taking advantage of it,
We may not be damned in your Justice.
Put your searchlight on our heart, that we may see ourselves as we truly are
And thus come to You for a bath unto purity.
We make our prayers, through Christ our Lord.
Amen.

CHAPTER 13

THE SACRAMENT OF MATRIMONY

The Church, the body of Christ, is also a family of God's people made up of smaller family units which fundamentally is based on the union of a man and a woman. It thus seems most appropriate to me that we discuss that sacrament that gives the grace to live well the family life, that is, the sacrament of Matrimony.

The practice of marriage has been and can be traced even to the very beginning of humanity, in actual fact, the creation of Man as male and female gives a natural reason to the union of one with the other, nevertheless, the formal sacramental description of marriage came at a somewhat later date (about 1000AD), even though Christian marriage has been practiced before thence. The teaching of the Church is based on the fact that Christ elevated marriage to a higher level, with its foundation being in the original intent of God (Cf. Mk 10:6-9).

Note the addition of Jesus; ...what therefore God has joined together, man must not put asunder. In this statement is contained some intrinsic points, following from the fact that marriage SHOULD be between a man and a woman, that determines the sacramental nature of marriage. Firstly, there is the fact that it is God who joins them, the man and woman, together. Yes, this is the basic reason for marriage, that it is not just a natural fusion of two adults of different sexes, but a sacred union with God as the principal witness.

On the other hand, there is the INSEPARABLE nature of this union - let no one put asunder. This second requirement gives the need for the first, for we all know that it could be very difficult for us as men and women with our selfish tendencies to keep to this, thus, we see more and more the need for God's grace which makes us ask for His presence in the union. From the above, we are able to see the properties of marriage, namely: UNITY and INDISSOLUBILITY.

Having known the properties, there is also a need for us to consider the Ends of Marriage, that is, for what reason do we essentially enter into marriage. This will help us to continually re-examine ourselves, considering whether we are still on the path.

The teaching of the Church is that the ends of marriage consist of Communion of life and Procreation, such that any union which is not open to any of these is outside the scope of marriage. The communion of life could be considered as a bringing together of the two properties of marriage, unity and indissolubility. This means that any marriag entered into without the intention of being together (of the couple) and for life is certainly not worthy of the sacrament of Matrimony. Examples of such abound in the makeup unions for specific civil purposes which abound nowadays in our world.

Furthermore, as regards Procreation, it is meant that for the sacrament of Matrimony to be valid, it must be open to life. In other words any union which has a pre-condition of childlessness cannot be a valid situation for the reception of the Sacrament of Matrimony in the Church. The reason for this is in the fact that all the sacraments are channels of grace and as such cannot act contrary to the nature of Christ, who is the Giver of grace.

Note the use of the word - Procreation! The word reproduction has not been used because it does not necessarily include responsibility for the offspring, as every lower animal and even plants reproduce to give continuation to the existence of the specie. More than this, in the sacrament of Matrimony, we talk of procreation, which is a pointer to taking part as co-creators in the work of God who is the Creator, and thus, a constant reminder of the responsibility that must be taken by the parents, on and for the child. This responsibility, first of all involves the care and education of the child brought forth in the family.

This sacrament is of such importance because it grants grace for the sustenance of family life, which in turn is the basis of the society. The many pointers to the relationship between God and Israel, Christ and the Church and the use of many parables of wedding feast as an explanation for God's kingdom, show how important this sacrament is and should be taken. Above all, the fact that Christ Jesus worked His first sign in the wedding feast of Cana (Jn. 2:1ff), illustrates the grace received when Christ is invited to one's wedding, together with His mother and the disciples (an image of the presence of the entire Church- Christ, the Head and Mary and the disciples, as members of the Body).

LET US PRAY

Father in heaven, You created man and woman
And willed that the two be united in marriage
For communion and procreation in Your presence
Thus bringing forth human family that reflects Your Trinitarian Commu-
nion.
Today, this intention of Yours is suffering in the hands of man,
As Your will is being distorted in many ways
That tends towards the destruction of family life and thence society.
By the intercession of the Holy Family of Nazareth,
Help us to come back to our senses and follow Your directives for us,
Grant peace to families passing through physical, emotional,
psychological, economical and spiritual tumult
Help young men and women to choose rightly with Your wisdom,
Open the womb of married mothers looking up to You for fruits of the
womb.
Bless our families and make us points of blessing to others.
Jesus, Mary, Joseph, intercede for our families.
Amen.

CHAPTER 14

HOLY ORDERS

In this chapter, dear friends we shall be taking a look at the Sacrament of Holy Orders; the sacrament that makes available an essential material for the other sacraments! What exactly do I mean by this statement? Christ, it is who instituted all the sacraments as a sign of His continuous stay with His body the Church (Cf. Matt 28:20), but in making this a physical continuation and not just mystical, He called and appointed a group of men (12 in number) out of His numerous disciples comprising of both male and female. These men, he called APOSTLES - a term that means being sent out, in the name of the Master. To this group of men, Christ Jesus gave the authority to baptize (Cf. Matt 28:19ff), to make present anew the sacrifice of Calvary (Matt 26:26ff, Lk 22:19, 1 Cor 11:24), to forgive sins (Cf. Jn 20:21ff), to heal the sick (Jm 5:4), make present the reign of the Holy Spirit (Cf. Acts 8:14-17, 9:17, Heb 6:2) and witness to the union of man and woman in Holy Matrimony (Cf. Jn 2:1-3). All these He did, above all when He ordained them as priests of the New Covenant in the upper room, during the last supper.

The idea of a priest, points to the reality of sacrifice and thus the reason why we cannot talk of the office of the priesthood without the offering of sacrifice and in the old covenantal idea of the priesthood, the sacrifice of blood stands as the optimum sacrifice of reconciliation between God and man and this sacrifice must be offered by the priests alone. Thus the scriptures say 'there is no forgiveness of sin without the shedding of blood' (Cf. Lev 7:11, Heb 9:22). In the New Covenant, instead of the blood of goats and rams and bulls, The Lord Jesus Christ offered Himself as the Lamb of God without blemish, whose blood pleads more insistently than Abel's (Cf. Jn 1:29, Heb 12:24), and He gave this group of men the authority to keep offering the same sacrifice in His memory.

It is here that the sacrament of Holy Orders came into existence and by the act of laying on of hands, the unbroken succession has continued even till our days. Here, I wish to emphasize two facts; the first is the intimate link that exists between the sacrament of Holy Orders and the Holy Eucharist and the second has to do with the idea of the Priesthood in relation to Sacrifice and Altar.

Now, we have been talking of Holy Orders and not Order because there are levels within this sacrament, such that the order of episcopate (Bishops) is different from the priesthood (Priests) and from diaconate (Deacons). The three make up the Holy Orders.

Thus, the sacrament of Holy Orders confers the grace on baptized men for the continuation of Christ's priesthood, explaining why priests are said to act in Persona Cristi when they preside over the celebrations of the Sacraments, for actually, it is Christ Himself who continues His saving actions through the instrumentality of the men who have been ordained into the Orders (be they bishops-the Pope is a bishop and captain of bishops, priests or deacons). Together with the sacraments of baptism and confirmation, this sacrament of Holy Orders confers an indelible mark on the soul and as such can only be received once! As such, even though a priest can be dispensed of his obligations as a priest, he remains a priest forever, as it is said at every ordination; You are a Priest forever like Melchizedek of old.

Finally, we need to note that each level of the sacraments confers special graces, for example, the grace to preach, baptize and witness the sacrament of matrimony granted to deacons, the ability to offer the Eternal Sacrifice of the Mass and absolve sins granted to priests and the special grace giving to bishops to ordain, confirm, teach and lead his flock, even to the point of dying as Christ died for the Church.

LET US PRAY

Lord Jesus Christ,
You chose Your apostles to continue Your saving work on earth,
And continue even till our day to call men into this ministry
Through the instrumentality of the Sacrament of Holy Orders.
Grant the grace of fidelity to those You have called
That loving You and Your body, the Church,
They may continue to lead Your people along the path of righteousness.
May Your Church never lack holy priests, who will continue to win souls
for the growth of Your kingdom here on earth.
We make our prayers through the holy name of Jesus Christ, The Lord.
Amen.

CHAPTER 15

ANOINTING OF THE SICK

In the last seven chapters, dear brothers and sisters, we have been discussing the actions of Jesus that perpetuate His presence with His Church and to which we are called to frequent as a response of faith. Here, we shall move a step further in considering the sacrament of Anointing of the Sick. In this sacrament, we come in actual contact with Christ the Eternal Doctor whose main reason for dwelling with us is for restoration - be it spiritual, physical and psychological. In the course of history, this sacrament at a point has been over stressed as a sacrament of preparation for death and thus given the nomenclature of Extreme Unction!

From the witness of the Apostles, this sacrament was not intended to just be for those who are at the point of death. In actual fact, any and every occasion of serious sickness is counseled to a request for this sacrament;

> *Is anyone among you sick? Let him call for the elders of the Church, and let them pray over him, anointing him with oil in the name of the Lord; and the prayer of faith will save the sick man, and the Lord will raise him up and if he has committed any sins, he will be forgiven (cf Jm 5:14-15).*

The fact of this passage from the letter of St. James, which can be considered as a furtherance of the promise of Jesus to His disciples that they will lay hands on the sick and such shall be healed (cf Mk 16:16ff) is a clear manifestation of Jesus' mission of restoration.

As of every other sacrament, it is expected that the recipient of this sacrament of healing is a baptized Christian and the reason is not far-fetched, since in Baptism, we take a public decision to belong to Jesus, and the prayer for healing is actually in that single Name which saves. This statement above does not mean that yet to be baptized persons cannot be prayed with for healing, but such prayers are not sacramental and should not be thus portrayed!

In many instances, the sacrament of Anointing of the Sick is preceded by the Sacrament of Reconciliation (cf. previous chapter), in such a way that the barriers of sin will be removed for healing and restoration to take place (cf. Mk 2:1-12). And it is usually followed by the sacrament of the Holy Eucharist. The oil used for the anointing of the sick in this sacrament is the oil blessed during the rite of the blessing of oil in the Mass of Holy Chrism by the bishop in unity with all his priests. Thus, the faith is that of the entire Church who believes that Christ is the great Healer.

Should a priest then be called? This could be our thought in instances of grave illnesses because we are still afraid that the sacrament will 'send our beloved across'. It is important for us to note always that the primary intention of this sacrament is the physical healing of the recipient, even before it prepares the soul for whatever may be the will of the Father. So, why should the priest not to be called? In fact, he should be called in earnest! Another fact to note is that we are not to abuse this sacrament by receiving it for every instance of headache and fatigue - the teaching of the Church is that the sacrament be administered as soon as any one of the faithful begins to be in danger of death from sickness or old age. As in every gift of the Lord for His Church, faith is required in the recipient, not because the Lord cannot heal without the faith of the recipient, but much more as a loving trust of His ever presence reality with us.

LET US PRAY

Father in heaven,
You sent your Son our Lord Jesus Christ to reveal Your care for us.
To restore us to the state of wholeness and complete health.
Send upon Your Church, a new consciousness
Of this sacrament of healing, which You have given unto Her,
That both the ministers and the recipients
May trustingly approach Your throne of mercy,
Asking for healing, liberation and restoration for all who are sick.
We pray today for every sick person who is connected to us
That by the merit of this sacrament, and the faith of Your Church,
They may be healed in body and spirit.
We make our prayer through Christ our Lord. Amen.

CHAPTER 16

CLOSING HINTS

Having made an attempt towards a better understanding of the sacraments which draw us to celebrations (frequenting) God's presence, we shall end this part with what I refer to as closing hints as regards the sacraments. They are actually things or issues we have earlier referred to in the course of discussing the sacraments which possibly were not explicitly stated or on the other hand were not taken notice of, by the reader.

1) The Sacraments are outward signs of inward graces, ordained by Jesus Christ.

2) The GATEWAY sacrament is the sacrament of BAPTISM; without it, no other sacrament is possible. It is the sacrament that makes us Christians and members of the Church.

3) The sacraments of Baptism, Confirmation and Holy Eucharist make up the sacrament of initiation; meaning that one is not yet a 'full-fledged' Catholic in the absence of any.

4) The EUCHARIST is the source and summit of our Christian life. Every other sacrament turns towards it.

5) The sacraments of Reconciliation, Anointing of the Sick and the Eucharist are sacraments of healing.

6) The sacraments of Holy Orders and Matrimony, Confirmation together with the Eucharist make up the sacraments at the service of communion or in another word the sacraments of mission.

7) The sacraments of Baptism, Confirmation and Holy Orders confer indelible mark on the soul of the recipient.

8) The Sacraments act 'Ex opere operato' literally meaning by the very act of the action being performed. Nevertheless, this will imply that the action is performed by the right person, within the right context, using the right form!

9) The celebration of the Sacraments is also called Liturgy, that is, an action of Christ, undertaken by the Church, His Body, in which every member has his/her role to play!

10) Christianity without Sacraments could be likened to 'a football pitch without players'

11) Every sacrament needs to be well and adequately prepared for! It is always an opportunity to meet with the Divine!

12) The Sacraments are the Seven Spiritual Wonders! Make effort to understand them better!

Lastly, I want to appreciate you for taking the pain to follow this part which has to do with celebrating, that is, frequenting our faith. In the next part, we shall treat the aspect of Faith Lived. May God in His infinite mercy, grant us the grace of better understanding of our faith and may our light of faith continue to shine for others to see. We ask this through Christ our Lord. Amen.

PART III
FAITH LIVED

CHAPTER 17

FAITH LIVED: INTRODUCTION

One of my most favorite passages of the Bible has been the narration of the Transfiguration of our Lord Jesus Christ (cf. Matt 17:1-13, Mk 9:1-9). The reason for this interest lies in the request of Peter to build three tents and the accompanying implicit reply of Jesus that they cannot remain ever there! It is actually like saying 'though it is interesting staying on the mount of transfiguration, but sorry, we have to go down/return to the valley of reality'. Faith is meaningless if it is not lived - the same fact that is always expressed at the end of every Mass; 'the Mass is ended, let us go in the peace of the Lord', which means, let us go and live out the grace we have received in our encounter with Christ. As put by St. James, 'faith, if it is without work is dead' (cf. Jm 2:17)

It is from this thought that we begin this part of our reflection on Faith Lived. Without mincing words, it is in living the faith that we make the greatest and most touching profession of the faith which is celebrated. It can be argued that faith lived takes us properly to the level of love, for the mere fact that it is relational and essentially concerns the other. If there is any fundamental problem of religion, it is in the fact that adherents of religion make a distortion between faith and life. They make particular professions but exhibit a mode of living that is completely different to the profession. Thus there is a visible tension in those who ordinarily would have opted for the religion. This kind of tension it was that led a person like Mohandas Ghandi to say; 'I like your Christ, but I do not like your Christians, your Christians are so much unlike Christ'.

Faith in itself cannot be shown because it is an abstract noun, but when it goes to the level of love, it becomes visible, for love is both a noun and a verb. This explains the reason why it is the name of God (cf. 1 Jn 4:8) and the mandate of Christians (cf. Jn 15:12). Thus, whatever faith we claim to have, amounts to nothing in the absence of love, for if at all it exists, it remains and ends with us and cannot be spread.

So, how do we make our faith living? Living in the sense of being active, loving! Our procession in this part will begin from the Decalogue which is a set of commandments given by God that are meant to be observed by whoever claim to be His follower; but much more, it will be a gradual movement from restriction from acting to a mandate to act.

LET US PRAY

Lord God, You are Love itself, and You called us to live in love.
Many a time, our lives do not correspond to Your call
Help us to grow in the life of love
That our faith, which we profess and celebrate
May come to be lived in You and with our brothers and sisters,
To the greater glory of Your name.
We ask this, through Christ our Lord. Amen.

CHAPTER 18

WHO IS MY MOTIVATING FORCE?

The Decalogue, also known as the Ten Commandments, is a set of precepts recorded by the Bible to have been given by God to Moses on Mount Sinai. It is meant to serve as a guideline for the Israelites in their relationship with God and with one another. Till date, this set of precepts continues to be a yardstick for adherents of Judaism and Christianity in their search to act according to the will of God. Our reflection on these precepts begins here from the very first of them all as recorded in Exodus 20:2-6, and this will be done in three parts:

1) *I am The Lord your God, who brought you out of the land of Egypt, out of the house of bondage:* Have you ever wondered why this commandment, which could be seen as a summary of the entire ten begins by a self-introduction of God? It is actually to put us in perspective, to confirm the relationship that exists between us and the Lawgiver - who is this that is talking to me? And He answered 'I am The Lord your God'. Again, the question continues; 'which Lord? (A reference to the possibility of many lords!) We should not lose sight of the fact that the word lord means master, and so He answered once again; the One who brought you from the land of Egypt, the land of bondage. Do I hear you say you have never been to Egypt, let alone of being taken out of the country? Maybe you are right in a way, but can you say in the same way that you have never been in bondage? Now the One talking is the same who has delivered us from the power of darkness and brought us into His own wonderful light (cf. Col 1:13), the same One who on the day of our baptism called us sons and daughters. The One to whom we have vowed our allegiance and in whose presence there is freedom (cf. 2 Cor 3:17). Unless you know Him for who He is, the other parts of the ordinance becomes meaningless, so, again ask yourself; 'Do I know now who is addressing me?

2) *You shall have no other god before me:* Attention! If you have come to the realization of whom He is, do you think it necessary to be told to cling to Him and not put any other god before Him? What are these other gods? They are all those things in which/whom we

put our trust and hope (cf. Ps 20:7). You may think you have no other god before The Lord, but then, you say you cannot worship The Lord until you are rich. Do you not see that riches has become your god? It is the ground of our existence that motivates us to action, so every time you act, a simple sincere question of 'what is motivating my action? will tell you who your god is. This second part is a call to us to love The Lord above every other thing.

3) *You shall not make for yourself a graven image, any likeness of anything that is in the heaven above, or that is in the earth beneath, or that is in the water under the earth; you shall not bow down to them or serve them....:* In continuation of His admonition, The Lord asks of us not to allow ourselves to be the source of breaking this precept - 'do not make for yourself a graven image'. This admonition is very necessary because many easily fall for the creation of their own hands, even though in a very subtle manner, it arrests all their attention and make them forget God. How many times have we tried like the people of old to build for ourselves 'a city and tower whose top may reach unto heaven...? Have you ever considered how a little material possession such as the mobile phone can take the place of God in our lives? Many consider this part of the commandment as restraining us from making any form of imagery and thus attack the Church for the use of statues. In response to this, I will like to say that what this commandment is warning us of is anything that will take our mind and attention off God as the Prime Motivator of our actions, and not what will attract us to Him (cf. Num 21:8, Ex 25:18-21, 1 kg 6:23-28, Eze 41:17-25).

Do you notice the fact that this first commandment has given the reasons for our existence? Our simple catechism teaches us that we are created to know, to love and to serve God in this life, so as to be eternally happy with Him in the life to come. Are you able to see these in the first commandment?

LET US PRAY

Father, You have revealed Yourself to us in Your Son,
Give us the grace to know You as our God and by so doing,
May we come to love You above everything, not just by words of mouth
But much more by our mode of living,
So that in our serving You, many more may come to believe in You
We make our prayer through Your Son our Lord Jesus Christ,
Who lives and reigns with You and the Holy Spirit,
One God forever and ever. Amen.

CHAPTER 19

WHAT IS IN A NAME?

One of my amazements in recent times is the kind of names that people give to their children. Not too long ago, a couple who was so used to pinging on blackberry phone, named their newly born son, Ping! If that happened a little far from us, we all would have heard some funny names that kept us questioning the motives behind giving such names. Whatever the name is, one basic fact is that names give identity, it differentiates a being from another and has a metaphysical import of bringing to consciousness, the reality it represents. Following from this, it would not be a thing of surprise that the second commandment of the Decalogue exhorts us against using the name of the Lord in vain - You shall not take the name of the Lord your God in vain, for the Lord will not leave him unpunished who takes His name in vain - (cf. Ex 20:7).

Respect for God's name, thence follows logically as a manifestation of the respect we have for God Himself. Wait a minute, can we boldly say we give the required respect and honour to God by our use of His name? It is almost a common, everyday occurrence now, that we use the name of God for false oaths - in this case, I will not only be making reference to our political leaders, but to all of us in general as homo politicus, how many times have we used the name of God to deceive people in business, in studies, even in friendship matters!

The modern day Religious Deception cannot be overlooked in this disregard for the Most Holy Name of God. Many so called religious leaders are nothing but actors, tricksters and magicians, who employ the name of God for deception. If these are guilty of misuse of God's name, much guiltier are those who unguardingly fall under their deceits, for these, in an imprudent search for worldly good, turn the name of God to a magical wand which for example, grants success without studies! I am tempted to also note here the modern day unnecessary abbreviation of God's name which is becoming so habitual to many of us and shows a great disregard for God's name. Such abbreviations have led us to seeing Christmas as Xmas, In Jesus name as IJN to mention a few. If only we know how precious the name of God is, we shall weep daily for the disrespect we accord to it.

Using in vain the name of the Lord extends to a misuse of holy objects and places. We only need to ask ourselves in what manners we have brought dishonour to the name of the Lord. In actual sense, a fake living of our Christian life is a misuse of His name, for in relation to Him are we called Christians. If in actual fact, we know Him whom we worship, it is doubly certain that we shall not attempt in any way to bring dishonour to His name or to use it in any way banal.

LET US PRAY

Father in heaven, holy is Your name!
Help us to always keep this in our minds,
To remember that by our baptism, we have been consecrated to you.
Enlighten us to realize always that Your name is to be kept holy,
That by our lives, we may testify to this
And avoid any and every instance of bringing dishonour to You
By an irreverent use of Your name.
We ask this, through Christ our Lord. Amen.

CHAPTER 20

KEEPING HOLY THE LORD'S DAY.

Man's desire for rest, like every one of his legitimate action is as a consequence of God's rest. This is to say that because God rested on the seventh day after having created heaven and earth, man also is entitled to a decent rest after labour. Nevertheless, the precept of the third commandment is much more about keeping holy the Sabbath, with rest being a means of achieving this.

Remember the sabbath day to keep it holy. Six day you shall labour; but the seventh day is a Sabbath to the Lord; in it you shall not do any work (Ex 20:8-10).

To rest is to dwell with the Lord (cf. Heb 4:5), a reference to the perception of man's work after having been driven out of the garden of Eden as a toil (Gen 3:18-19), because it is to be done away from God's presence. Thus, the precept forbids every and any work that will take our mind away from God, for there lies no rest, but does not forbid the works of love (Mk 2:27-28), for God is love and those who dwell in love, dwell in God (cf. 1 Jn 4:8).

It will be a pleasant thing to start explaining the shift from the Jewish Sabbath to the Christian day of The Lord, but that is not the aim of this little piece. On the other hand, it is expedient for us to note that we are called to live every day in God's presence, but much more, that day, on which we are redeemed from the curse of Eden and brought back essentially into a living relationship with God by the virtue of the resurrection of the Lord (cf. 1 Cor 15:14ff). Since God rested and was refreshed on the seventh day, man too ought to rest and should let others especially the poor be refreshed! (Cf. CCC 2172). The question is; are we able to say that our daily works bring us into a deeper communion with God or farther from Him? Are we not going away farther from the living God and attaching ourselves more to mammon (Lk 16:13). Much more than this, does the day of our redemption sound any difference into our ears? Do we see it as a call to manifesting our sense of gratitude to a God who so loved us to the point of dying for us by worshipping Him?

Keeping holy the Sabbath does not stop on Sundays alone, but we must go further to see every day as what it is, a day of experiencing newly the love of God and showing the same unto others (cf. Lam 3:22-23). Nevertheless, we are called upon on Sundays to make a public, visible and outward worship unto the Lord, to sanctify the beginning of the week and in a way, a recalling of the beginning of our new birth in the Lord. We listen to the Lord as He speaks to us in His word, and nourish us with His body and blood, and as everyone becomes what he eats, we are called to become Him of whose body and blood we have been nourished. Thus, as the priest says at the end of the Mass that we '...go in peace', we are being reminded to take the fruit of the Mass to sanctify our weekly activities.

How do we make use of the day of the Lord? Do we remember at all that it belongs not unto us, or like the prodigal son, we take our inheritance and spend it on life of debauchery? Our observance of the Sabbath will amount to nothing, unless we come to the awareness that it is meant to bring us into deeper intimacy with Christ, and should bring forth from us works of love by which we shall sanctify the entire week, for all days are the Lord's, and as such, meant to be kept holy.

LET US PRAY

Father in heaven,
Every day of our life is your creation
And gift unto us, as our inheritance
Help us come to this awareness, and as such
Use each day to the greater glory of Your holy name.
Make us come to a deeper experience of Your presence
With us as we come into Your house to worship You,
And may the fruit of our worship be visible in our lives afterwards.
We make our prayers, through Christ our Lord. Amen.

CHAPTER 21

OBEDIENCE TO PARENTS AND ELDERS AS IN THE LORD.

Honour your father and your mother, that your days may be long in the land which the Lord your God gives you (Ex 20:12).

Have you ever noticed that this commandment is one of the only two which were spoken of in positive terms? Do you know that it is the only one that has a promise attached to it? It is not that surprising as we shall come to see later that the boundary commandments are the only two that were given in positive terms, that is, the third commandment which invites us to keep holy the Lord's day, ending the set of precepts that talk directly of our relationship with God and this fourth commandment which begins our relationship with one another on the human plane. Another point worthy of observation is the fact that immediately after God, come our parents, and by extension all those who are in positions of authority over us. Why?

It is God, who is the author of our lives, without Him, we are nothing! Nevertheless, this life, He bequeath unto us through the instrumentality of our parents. Such that none of us can ever claim to have come to the world alone and without the help of another. If our parents have cooperated with God in giving us life, then they by every right deserve to be honoured (cf. Sir 7:27-28, Prov. 6:20-22, 13:1). Many children nowadays think they have a hundred and one reasons for not honouring their parents, but the fundamental question is 'would we even have had all these reasons if we had no life in the first instance?

Notwithstanding, we should not lose sight of the fact that this commandment came only after the precepts that talk of our relationship with God, which in a way tell us that God comes by right before our parents. Thus, St. Paul admonishes us to obey our parents as in the Lord (cf. Eph 6:1), which in a way tells us that the only time we could be justified in not carrying out our parents' directives and wills is when such are contrary to God's will!

By extension, the Church teaches us further that this law includes also all those who are in positions of authority over us, for all authority is of God (cf Rom 13:1, Heb 13:17). As such, our lived faith could be considered from the perspective of the honour we give to our parents (cf. Mk 7:10-13), and it brings unto us a blessing that is ordained by God Himself (Sir 3:2-6, 12-13). While the scriptures require obedience and honour from children to parents, it beckons also on parents to give necessary instruction and discipline to their children (cf. Sir 30:1-3, Eph 6:4). Necessary it is to point out that many parents today fail in this responsibility, sometimes for a wrong understanding of what love is; forgetting that love does not rejoice in wrongdoing (cf. I Cor 13:6). It is of utmost importance, that parents cater physically and spiritually for their children and thereby set their feet on the path of righteousness.

LET US PRAY

Our Father in heaven,
You reveal to us always what it means to be a parent,
Loving us with abundant mercy and yet punishing our offences;
In this way, You prune us until we bear fruits that will last.
Help parents to take a leave from You, and adequately bring up their chil-
dren in accordance with Your will.
Your Son, our Lord Jesus Christ,
When He came to dwell among us, gave us also an example
Of the obedience required from children to their parents;
Following His example, help us to live obediently with our parents and all
who are in positions of authority over us, and to honour them, that our
lives may be fruitful on the land which You have given to us.
We make our prayers, through Christ our Lord. Amen.

CHAPTER 22

THE SANCTITY OF LIFE.

From the length to the breath of the earth, east to west and north to south, there is just the same battle taking place, involving two cultures; the culture of life against the culture of death! It is a pitiable condition that there are many more in the 'Death Culture' team than in the team for life. In other words, many more opt for the devil whose mission is to steal, to kill and to destroy (cf Jn 10:10a), than those who are on the side of Jesus, who has come that man should have life in abundance (cf. Jn 10:10b). The commandment of God is very clear as regards this; You Shall Not Kill (Cf. Ex 20:13), but what is not clear to many is the many sides of taking others' life.

From the quotation given above, we can deduce that anything that reduces the sacredness and dignity of life is a transgression against this precept, for the intention of the Son of God is that they may have life in ABUNDANCE, not just surviving, but actually living. Ranging from the physical taking of life, at whatever stage of its existence, to a deprivation of basic necessities that make life worthy of being lived, whoever engages in such, holds not the sanctity of life and thus belongs to the camp of the culture of death.

Closely linked to this act of taking life are the emotions of anger and envy, which may drive man to the point of doing the abominable. Such can be seen in the case of Cain (cf. Gen 4:3-8). In our modern world, added to this is an unholy egoistic tendency which thinks solely of itself and never of others; the type that ascribes to self what others need to make a living for themselves (cf. I Kg 21: 1-14). In other words, being blind to the basic needs of others while I live in superabundance (cf. Lk 16:19-31). The unholy murder of innocent souls through acts of abortion cannot be overlooked in this discussion, neither can the act of inciting others to anger, acts of terrorism, thuggery to mention a few go without mention. In all of these, the precept of the Lord is firm and direct (cf. Gen 9:5-6). The constant question that ought to be on our lips and in our hearts is; "Am I on the side of Life or a messenger of death? Our daily living should be always a challenge to make available unto others a better life and anything short of this, puts a question mark on our claim to a life of faith.

LET US PRAY

Lord God,
You are the Author and Giver of life.
Help us to know the truth that life is holy,
And as such, its sanctity is to be upheld always.
Make us know the way to walk in this truth
And propagate the fullness of life wherever we find ourselves
We make our prayers through Your Son, our Lord Jesus Christ,
Who Himself is the Way, the Truth and the Life,
And lives in union with You and the Holy Spirit,
One God forever and ever. Amen.

CHAPTER 23

A CALL TO CHASTITY

The word chastity refers to the state or quality of refraining from every sexual act that is considered contrary to morality. Thus, in guiding our path along the path of righteousness, the precepts of the Lord bid us to live in chastity by saying: "You shall not commit adultery" (Ex 20:14).

This ordinance of the Lord can be considered as one of the most commonly transgressed in contemporary times. God, who created man as male and female (cf. Gen 1:27), intends our sexuality to be a gift which is to be appreciated and used for His glory and thus, any denial of this sexuality or misuse of it, falls within the acts which this commandment forbids.

In a recent discussion with a group of youths, I was asked by one of the participants: "Fr. how is it possible to sin in God? If God is Love, how does making love become a sin?" An intelligent question you may want to say, but then a closer look will show where the question is fundamentally faulty. Undeniably, God is love! But the question is 'what is love and how do we recognize it? Scripturally, our immediate reference to what love is, will be the song used by St. Paul in the acknowledgement of love (Cf. I Cor 13). In this song, St. Paul begins by showing us the possibility of actions which ordinarily ought to be positive but rendered negative by the absence of love (verse 1-3). He continues to give the qualities of love which include perseverance/long suffering, not seeking its own and rejoicing in the truth (verse 4-6).

Going further, we will say that the difference between love and lust is the orientation of both: while love is others' oriented, lust on the other hand thinks of self-gain; love is patient and persevere, while lust is impatient and thinks of immediate pleasure; love is open to life, lust on the other hand is not! Taking the last mentioned end of love as in contrast to lust, we can then ask further questions as regard the issues being treated; when we talk of love making, are we thinking of the other? Are we patient or seek immediate pleasure? Is our love making open to life?

If the answers to the above questions are in the positive, the next consideration is 'Why is it not rightly done? Since love does not rejoice in wrong doing, why do we not get married rightly and then 'make love' rightly?

As earlier said, this precept is not only against a misuse of sexuality, but also every abuse of it. Thus, every denial of sexuality, that is, the gift of our masculinity or femininity, is a sin against this precept. We shall not fail to mention the many avenues in contemporary times which encourage the transgression of this precept, ranging from the mass media promotion of arbitrary sex, pornography, indecent dressing manners, to general break down of societal values and our newly found consumerism culture.

As a mechanism to avoid falling into this sin, the scriptures request of us to flee (cf. I Cor. 6:18). Is it not surprising that not even against the devil did the scripture ask us to run away from? Instead, we are asked to stand against the devil and he will flee from us (cf. James 4:12). But as regards the sin against the sixth commandment, we are asked to flee, meaning to avoid every occasion that may lead to such.

LET US PRAY

Holy God, Holy Mighty One, Holy Immortal One,
To You we come in our human weakness
But with full knowledge that we are created in Your image,
We seek to become holy in Your likeness.
Help us to overcome every deceptive call of the devil,
That living in purity of body, mind and spirit,
We may come to experience more Your ever present love for us
We ask this through Christ our Lord. Amen.

CHAPER 24

LET THE RICH LIVE SIMPLY...

As we continue with this part on Faith Lived, let us reflect in this chapter, on an understanding of what it means when we are referred to as stewards of Christ. Indeed we have all been given different portions; personal though they are, but for the common good. So we consider the seventh precept of the Lord as given through Moses, which admonishes us not to unlawfully take what does not belong to us: "Thou shall not steal" (cf. Ex 20:15).

What does it mean to steal? This question seems so clear to everybody, that we are much more likely to have everybody answering it. To steal is to take or appropriate to oneself what belongs to another, either by trick, secretly or by force. As much as this answer is correct, what remains somehow cloudy to many is the term "what belongs to another". For that reason, it is necessary to trace down to the origin, the ownership of what is.

In the Genesis account of creation, a vivid account is given of the fact that man is the last point of God's creation and to him is given the responsibility of taking care of the earlier created realities (cf. Gen 1:1-31). From this account, a truth to be deduced is that in its ultimacy, everything that there is, belongs to God, while man has been chosen by God to be the steward or the caretaker of everything. This aforementioned fact does not contradict the fact of the appropriation of property through right means for the reason of maintaining the dignity and freedom of man, and for aiding him to meet his basic needs, and that of those who are put under his care. Having said this, we can mention two paths to stealing which must be guarded against. The first, is to take what belongs to the other, that which he needs for survival without his permission. The second is to unlawfully hoard what would have been beneficent to another, such that he becomes deprived and has to live in an undignifying manner!

Going deeper into each of the paths, the first will refer to all forms of illegal possession of another's property through acts such as business fraud, forcing up market prices, tampering with measuring scales, paying unjust salaries, buying others' property at ridiculous prices due to their hardship, reducing the quality of goods sold or services rendered, evading legal taxes, not paying for social services being rendered, laziness, lateness to work, using working hours to make calls and chat on Social Media or pinging and ingratitude (cf. Lev 19:35-36) to mention but a few.

On the other hand, every excessive possession of properties, knowledge not shared, food wasted are some of the ways of depriving others of a meaningful life to others who would have benefited from the excess had it been charitably shared. All these are examples of what the seventh commandment admonishes us against. It is a recalling of the fact that we are stewards and as such, should do the right thing at the right time, for blessed is the servant whom the Master finds doing the right thing when He returns (cf. Lk 12:45). It is a call to us all to live simply wherever we find ourselves, in order to make others, simply live.

LET US PRAY

Father in heaven,
We thank You for choosing us as stewards of what belong to You, help us
to rightly make use of Your gifts to us,
To give dignity and freedom to others around us.
Make us know that our lives are not measured by what we have,
But much more by who we are.
May we share justly Your gifts to us,
That so doing, we may construct for ourselves here on earth,
Eternal abodes in Your kingdom.
We ask this, through Christ our Lord. Amen.

CHAPTER 25

BEAR NOT FALSE WITNESS.

In the book of Deuteronomy (17:6) and the second letter of St. Paul to the Corinthians (13:1), we see a basis for making a thorough investigation into issues before we come with a judgement. The lack of such thorough inquiry has led in history to many irrational acts of injustice in the history of man. These are only discovered later when little or nothing can be done again to remedy the situation. At least we all know that even when the wound is healed, the scar remains!

Nevertheless, because of abuses, the precept of the Lord also warn us to be careful of the kind of testimonies that we give either in support of or against another, for when such is false, it becomes a sin against justice, a sin against truth. And as such, the eighth commandment requests of us, not to bear false witness against our neighbours.

You shall not bear false witness against your neighbour (cf. Ex 20:16)

Put in another way, this commandment is asking that we say only the truth about our neighbours, saying 'yes' when we mean 'yes' and 'no when we mean 'no'! Much more than that, it is requesting of us to say only what is necessary about the other and nothing more or less. How many times, have we been a party to spreading unfounded rumours as regard the other even when we have no proof of the certainty of what transpired? How many times have we depended on public opinion, forgetting that the majority is not always right, and we defame other people's character? How many times have we disregarded the dignity of the other and revealed what we know of him or her (even when such is true) without necessity, or before those we are not supposed to? Every time we do any of such acts, we transgress against the eighth commandment and deny Jesus our Lord, for He is the Truth!

When we make ourselves sources of unfounded rumours, how are we different from the chief priests who inspire in others the denial of Christ's resurrection, by asking them to say that His disciples came to take His body away (cf. Matt 28:11-15)?

When we depend on public opinion without searching for the truth of the matter diligently, how are we different from Pilate, who gave Jesus up to death just because of people's opinion (cf. Mk 15:1-15). And how different are we from Judas Iscariot when we sell others to their enemies even if we had said the 'truth'?

It is very true that we are called to witness to the truth, bearing in mind that the word witness indicates a firsthand or personal experience, but then, we should be cautious so as not to fall into the undoing of perjury, rash judgement, detraction or calumny!

LET US PRAY

Lord Jesus Christ,
You are the Truth, and it is in living in You that we are liberated.
Let Your light shine upon us, that we may see the stained part of our lives
Help us to know the truth of ourselves and others,
And in this truth, deal with others without destroying their dignity.
May we find joy in telling the truth always,
Unto Your glory and the good of our brothers and sisters.
Protect us from the deceptions of the devil; the father of all lies.
We ask this through Christ our Lord.
Amen.

CHAPTER 26

GUARD YOUR DESIRE

In this chapter dear reader, we shall be looking at the ninth and tenth commandments together for the reason that both are concerned about our desire of what belongs to another, though from different perspectives:

You shall not covet your neighbour's house, wife (husband), man/maidservant, ox, ass or anything that belongs to your neighbour. (Cf. Ex 20:17).

In this verse is contained both of the two precepts that warn against covetousness. The lexical definition of the word 'Covet', is to desire wrongfully, inordinately, or without due regard for the rights of others. Thus, these two commandments are separated by the object of the inordinate desire, that is, while the ninth commandment admonishes against carnal covetousness, the tenth on the other hand warns against coveting the material possessions of other.

As insignificant as these commandments may seem on the first look, they actually are the root leading to breaking other commandments! When the desire of man is not ordered rightly, it gives birth to innumerable vices (cf. Lk 6:45). For when we are filled with a wrong desire for what belongs to others, we are easily led to murder (cf. Gen 4:1-8), bearing false witness (cf. I kg 21:1ff), adultery (cf. 2 Sam. 11) and so on.

Every form of envy and jealousy are also part of offenses against this commandment. On the other hand, while it is wrong to unduly desire what belongs to others, it is also wrong to willfully incite others to having such desires (cf. Lk 17:1). Thus, every unnecessary flamboyancy which has the tendency of leading others to inordinate desires, is also to be avoided. Within this class of action are; unnecessary exposition of wealth, immodest dressing, self-aggrandizement and every action that may make the other have undue desires.

In actual fact, it can be said that these commandments call us to moderation in our mode of living for while we are called to appreciate God in others and even appreciate others for their abilities and talents. When intemperance creeps in, it leads us to acting against the will of God, thereby sinning and destroying the normal order of creation.

Father in heaven,
You are our Creator and Provider,
Help us to appreciate Your creation rightly,
That we may not be overcome by intemperance,
And thereby fall away from Your grace.
May we not be led into sin,
Through our inability to guard against our desires.
We ask this, through Christ our Lord. Amen.

CHAPTER 27

FAITH LIVED:
MOVING FROM DON'TS TO DO!

So far, we have dwelt on the need to live out our faith and as such, also considering the how. Nevertheless, we have been greatly concerned with the precepts given to Moses by God, which mark, or in another word spring us to live in a mode of achieving the likeness of God who created us in His image (cf. Gen 1: 26).

Unfortunately, many of us have been stuck just to this level of 'inactive morality'. While in itself, it is not a bad thing, I am of the view that it is meant for babies in the faith, to restrain them from acting in particular manners until they inculcate the habit of how to act (cf. I Cor. 3:2). It is the growth, the maturity which brings one to this new level that is found wanting in many of us Christians!

If we may ask again, what then is the new level? Is there a new set of precepts? In responding to the second question, I will readily say that there is not a new set of precepts; rather, there is a new understanding of the intentionality of the already existing set. It is the Decalogue, written in positive terms! A call to act, to do something and not just to refrain from acting.

In response to those who came to ask Him for the greatest of all the commandments; (a question that is filled with an inherent intention of reductionism, whereby one only does what he considers the most needed and leaves the others undone), Jesus gave two answers; love God and love your neighbours (cf. Matt 22:35-40).

Now, let us make some necessary observations on this passage of the scripture. Firstly, Jesus was asked, 'which is the greatest commandment? By its nature, this question requires an answer that refers to just one article (and which could it have been?). No wonder the question came from a lawyer! But in response, Jesus gave what looks like two answers on one side, and totally out of context on the other hand (for the two answers are not contained in the Ten Commandments).

Alas! None of these observations is totally correct, for in actual fact, Jesus only gave one answer, that has two sides. It is like a coin that has two faces but nevertheless remains just a coin, and to damage a side makes the coin unacceptable for transactions. Thus, the response of Jesus is: You shall love! To the observation of whether or not this commandment is contained in the Decalogue, it will be seen that, it is actually the spirit of every letter of Decalogue; for those who worship the Lord, worship Him in spirit and in truth (cf. Jn 4:24).

Thus, we are brought to the level of the matured Christianity which is a call to love. Love as a word is both a noun and a verb. In Christian living, we are called to a relation with Love as noun; for God is Love (cf. I Jn 4:8), in order to be able to love (verb) our neighbours (cf. Lk 10:25-37) and vice versa (cf. Matt 25:31-46). This is the one and only commandment of Christian living and it is only within this context that our faith, which we profess and celebrate, can be lived authentically.

LET US PRAY

O Love Incomprehensible,
To You we come this day in our frailty
We seek to find You and be built in You,
But we are not in any way worthy of Your presence,
Except by grace, You permit us.
Give us this grace, that we may experience You deeper in our lives.
As we experience You, instill in us the zeal,
To share You with others, by our mode of living,
That one day, together we may come to praise You for all eternity,
Having been blessed with the joy of knowing You here on earth.
We make our prayers, through Christ our Lord. Amen.

CHAPTER 28

CONCLUSION

In this booklet which came as an aftermath of the Year of Faith declared by Pope Benedict XVI from October 11, 2012 to November 24, 2013, I have in my own little way tried to make a simplification and exposition of what it means to Profess, Celebrate and Live the faith. The title of "Faith PLC" is actually meant to reflect this reality as the PLC is an acronym for Profess, Live and Celebrate!

I have done this work on weekly basis as a form of teaching on the Catholic Friends Forum and the St. Stephen Youth Ministry, where questions and contributions of members have prompted me to make further clarifications. In actual fact, the decision to put this work into print is borne out of the request of many members of these groups. As usual, my main target remains the youth of the Church, as many are being led astray by false teachers and prophets, as the prophet Hosea put it in his prophecy; my people perish for lack of knowledge (cf. Hosea 4:6)

It is my intention that as hope of the future which actually begins here and now, the youths will not only pick and read this booklet, but much more, shall allow it to act as a springboard unto digging deeper into the reasons for our faith, in such a way that we may be able to give answer to those who ask us for the reasons for the hope which we have in us! (Cf. 1 Pet 3:15). The Year of Faith might have ended, but its calls further still should be a challenge to all of us involved in Youth Apostolates and pastors of soul to dedicate valuable time to listening to youths as regards what issues they have in making the faith take flesh in their daily living. For if we fail to feed these lambs, we may be exposing them furthermore to the risk of wolves who lurk in hiding to hurt them.

This work has not pretended in any way to answer all the questions there are in the best possible way they could. But, it has initiated something, no matter how little that will instigate better dialogue and deeper search. I pray that the Holy Spirit will continue to enlighten us all to a better understanding of our faith, to the glory of God the Father. Amen.

Volume stampato da FCM printing
20010 - Marcallo con Casone (Mi)
nel 2014

In this small volume, the author gives a personal
experience of what faith is, showing how difficult
it is to describe a faith that is not expressed and
lived. The simple and practical illustrations of
the supposedly abstract contents of faith – in a
simple and direct language – make this book an
essential vademecum for everyone, especially young
Christians, who will soon realize that the faith can
be explained without any 'dull moment'. I strongly
recommend this book for all who want to go on a
journey of faith, seeking deeper understanding of the
content of our Christian faith, with a view to using
their life as a practical expression or testimony of
the faith they profess in our Lord Jesus.
Rev. Fr. Kenneth A. Adesina

In this simple but stunning work, Fr. Peter Akinola
expresses that, "the aim is for it to serve both as
a challenge for others to also share the faith and
as an insight to those searching for the reasons for
the hope they have in them." The reader will find
its depth in how well he communicates with a style
of writing which is straight to the point, and quite
down to earth. At particular points, one can tell what
next he will address, but the weaving of experience
and intuition, leaves one with no doubt about how
well Fr. Akinola himself has found wisdom in God's
revelation (Scripture and Tradition) and in the
teaching authority of the Church (Magisterium).
Hence not only does he sound convinced that the
faith professed ought to be lived and celebrated, this
conviction takes him to the height of putting it down
in this handy piece and presenting it to everyone
who lay his hands upon it a useful guide. Indeed this
book has its usefulness in every sense, for the faith,
especially in the pastoral ambience and precisely for
catechesis.
Fr. Martin Badejo
(Facoltà Teologica Settentrionale, Milan. Italy)